101 Things To Do With Canned Soup

101 Things To Do With Canned Soup

BY
DONNA KELLY AND
STEPHANIE ASHCRAFT

GIBBS SMITH

Gibbs Smith, Publisher
SALT LAKE CITY

First Edition
11 10 09 08 07   5 4 3 2 1

Published by
Gibbs Smith, Publisher
P.O. Box 667
Layton, Utah 84041

Orders: 1.800.835.4993
www.gibbs-smith.com

Designed by Kurt Wahlner
Printed and bound in Korea

Library of Congress Cataloging-in-Publication Data

Kelly, Donna.
  101 things to do with canned soup / Donna Kelly and Stephanie
Ashcraft. — 1st ed.
     p. cm.
  ISBN-13: 978-1-4236-0027-5
  ISBN-10: 1-4236-0027-4
  1. Quick and easy cookery. 2. Soups. I. Ashcraft, Stephanie. II.
Title. III. Title: One hundred and one things to do with canned
soup.

TX833.5.K45 2007
641.5'55—dc22

                                    2006102585

With gratitude to Jim, my eternal companion and best friend, whose Midwest roots have taught me appreciation for the many simple joys in life, including comfort food. For your hours of taste testing, critiquing and service as a prep chef, I am truly and eternally grateful.

—D.K.

This book is dedicated to college friends who have always inspired me to do my best. To Mike Owens, thank you for numerous hours of listening and for gentle correction when needed. To Aaron Kammerman, thank you for setting such a high standard for all of us to follow. To Ryan Bateman, thank you for being yourself and such a great friend. And finally, to my dear Jenny Bruner, thank you for all your prayers, love, faith and support throughout all these years! I love you all!

—S.A.

CONTENTS

Beef & Pork

Family Favorites

Breakfast or Brunch

Baked Goods

HELPFUL HINTS

I. Using canned soup as a convenience item is a smart way to make delicious and almost effortless meals quickly. Soups come in a wide variety, including health conscious and international recipes.

2. This book is designed to keep the number of ingredients to a minimum. Generally, the fewer the ingredients, the more important it is to use better-quality ingredients. Check soup labels to make sure they have the quality and quantity of ingredients that will work with your recipes.

3. For recipes that call for minced garlic, prepared jarred garlic may be used.

4. Cream of chicken, cream of onion, cream of mushroom, and cream of celery condensed soups can be used interchangeably in most recipes.

5. For lighter meals, use low-fat or light ingredients.

6. Generally, use canned soups that would be good enough to eat alone and are made with only water or milk added.

7. The first time you try baking a recipe, check the food 3–5 minutes before its minimum cooking time ends. Each oven heats differently, so cooking times can vary.

8. The sodium content of soups varies, so use salt carefully in recipes, adding only a little at a time and tasting as you go.

9. For an emergency dinner, try creating sauces using undiluted cans of condensed soups with fresh herbs, spices, and a few finely minced onions or garlic cloves to add flavor. Use sauces to flavor cooked meats, vegetables, and/or pastas.

I0. To make cleanup easier, spray baking pans with nonstick cooking spray before adding ingredients.

Appetizers

SOUR CREAM MEATBALLS

5 pounds	**fully cooked frozen Italian meatballs,** thawed
I can (10.5 ounces)	**cream of onion soup,** condensed
I can (10.5 ounces)	**cream of mushroom soup,** condensed
2 teaspoons	**minced garlic**
$^3/_4$ cup	**water**
I container (16 ounces)	**sour cream**

Place meatballs in a greased 5- to 7-quart slow cooker.

In a bowl, combine soups, garlic, and water. Pour soup mixture evenly over meatballs. Cover and cook on low heat for 3–4 hours until heated. Stir in sour cream during the last 30 minutes of cooking. Serve hot with toothpicks. Makes 20 servings.

SALSA NACHO CHEESE

1 pound **ground beef,** browned and drained
1 jar (16 ounces) **chunky salsa**
1 can (10.5 ounces) **tomato soup,** condensed
2 pounds **Velveeta cheese,** cubed

Combine all ingredients in a greased $3^1/_2$- to 5-quart slow cooker. Cook on high heat, stirring occasionally for 1 hour until cheese melts. Reduce heat to low or warm until ready to serve. Serve with tortilla chips. Makes 15 servings.

BAKED PEPPERONI DIP

$^1/_2$ pound **pepperoni,** cubed
I can (10.5 ounces) **cream of celery soup,** condensed*
I package (8 ounces) **cream cheese,** softened

Preheat oven to 350 degrees.

In a greased 8 x 8-inch baking pan, combine pepperoni, soup, and cream cheese. Bake 25 minutes, or until light brown and bubbly. Serve with toasted baguette slices, mini bagel halves, or breadsticks. Makes 6–8 servings.

*Cream of chicken or cream of mushroom soup can be substituted.

CREAMY CHICKEN DIP

I can (10–12.5 ounces) **chunk chicken,** drained and shredded
I can (14.5 ounces) **diced tomatoes with green chiles,**
with liquid
I package (8 ounces) **cream cheese,** softened
I can (10.5 ounces) **cream of chicken soup,** condensed
I can (10.75 ounces) **nacho cheese soup,** condensed

Combine all ingredients in a medium saucepan. Cook 20 minutes over medium heat, stirring constantly until bubbly. Serve with tortilla chips, French bread cubes, toasted baguette slices, or crackers. Makes 10–12 servings.

PORK CHILI DIP

1/2 pound	**cooked ham,** finely chopped
8 ounces	**Velveeta Mexican cheese,** cubed
1 can (10 ounces)	**diced tomatoes with green chiles,** with liquid
1 can (10.5 ounces)	**cream of mushroom soup,** condensed
1 can (4.25 ounces)	**chopped black olives,** drained
1 can (15 ounces)	**chili**

Combine all ingredients in a 3-quart saucepan. Cook over medium heat, stirring slowly until cheese is completely melted. Serve with tortilla chips or strips. Makes 10–12 servings.

VARIATION: This can also be made in a greased slow cooker over high heat. Once cheese is melted, reduce heat to low to serve.

CHEESY VARIATION: Add an extra 8 ounces Velveeta Mexican cheese.

BEEFY BEAN DIP

1 pound **ground beef,** browned and drained
1 can (10.75 ounces) **nacho cheese soup,** condensed
1 can (16 ounces) **refried beans**
1 jar (16 ounces) **hot salsa**
1 can (4 ounces) **diced green chiles**
1/2 pound **Velveeta cheese,** cubed

In a 3- to 4-quart saucepan, combine cooked beef, soup, beans, salsa, chiles, and cheese. Cook over medium heat, stirring every once in a while until melted and bubbly. Serve with tortilla chips or strips. Makes 10–12 servings.

VARIATION: For a hotter version, use jalapeno peppers in place of green chiles.

WORLD'S EASIEST CHEESE FONDUE

2 cans (10.75 ounces each)	**cheddar cheese soup,** condensed
1 can (12 ounces)	**evaporated milk**
1 teaspoon	**Worcestershire sauce**
1 teaspoon	**dry mustard**
$^1/_2$ cup	**white grape juice**
8 ounces	**Swiss or Havarti cheese,** grated
1 tablespoon	**flour**
8 to 10 cups	**cubed lightly steamed vegetables***
1 loaf	**French bread,** cut into cubes

In a medium saucepan, mix together soup, milk, Worcestershire sauce, dry mustard, and grape juice. Bring to a simmer over medium heat. Toss cheese with flour and then stir into pan; turn off heat. Pour into a fondue pot for serving. Serve warm with vegetables and bread for dipping. Makes 6–8 servings.

*Try using broccoli, cauliflower, zucchini, potatoes, and squash.

SAVORY SUN-DRIED TOMATO CHEESECAKE

1 1/2 cups	**crushed club crackers**
1/4 cup	**butter,** melted
1/4 cup	**grated Parmesan cheese**
2 packages (8 ounces each)	**cream cheese,** softened
1 can (10.75 ounces)	**cream of onion soup,** condensed
1/2 cup	**sour cream**
1 tablespoon	**lemon juice**
4	**large eggs**
1 jar (8 ounces)	**sun-dried tomatoes in oil,** drained

Preheat oven to 350 degrees.

In a bowl, mix together cracker crumbs, butter, and Parmesan cheese. Spread mixture in the bottom of a 9-inch springform pan.

In a separate bowl, mix cream cheese, soup, sour cream, lemon juice, and eggs with a mixer on medium-high speed. Finely mince tomatoes and add while mixing. Pour mixture on top of crust and bake 45–50 minutes, or until center is nearly set and top is lightly browned. Turn off oven and let sit 15 minutes before removing. Remove from oven and remove sides of pan. Bring to room temperature before serving. Spread on thin toasted slices of bagels or French bread to serve. Makes 10–12 servings.

SAVORY PESTO CHEESECAKE VARIATION: Replace sun-dried tomatoes with 1 jar (6 ounces) pesto.

SAVORY SMOKED SALMON CHEESECAKE VARIATION: Replace soup with cream of shrimp soup. Replace sun-dried tomatoes with 1 package (6 ounces) Nova Scotia–style smoked salmon, finely minced.

NEW ENGLAND CLAM DIP

I package (8 ounces)	**cream cheese,** softened
I can (15 ounces)	**New England clam chowder,** condensed
I teaspoon	**Worcestershire sauce**
I teaspoon	**grated horseradish,** or more to taste
I teaspoon	**white pepper**
3	**green onions,** thinly sliced with tops included
2 cans (6 ounces each)	**minced clams,** well drained

Stir together all ingredients until well blended and then pour into a small serving bowl. Refrigerate 2 hours or more. Serve chilled with chips. Makes $2^1/2$ cups.

BEAN AND BACON FONDUE

2 cans (11.5 ounces each) **bean with bacon soup,** condensed
1 envelope **taco seasoning**
1/2 cup **salsa**
1 cup **sour cream**
1/2 cup **grated cheddar cheese**

In a 2-quart saucepan, combine soup, taco seasoning, and salsa. Cook over medium heat until bubbly. Stir in sour cream and cheese. Cook an additional 2–3 minutes until hot. Serve with lightly toasted tortilla triangles, French bread cubes, and tortilla chips. Makes 6–8 servings.

ZESTY ROAST BEEF BITES

8 ounces **cream cheese,** softened
$^1/_2$ can (10.75 ounces) **cream of onion soup,** condensed
1 tablespoon **grated horseradish,** or more to taste
16 ounces **cooked deli roast beef,** sliced into
$^1/_8$-inch-thick slices

In a food processor, mix cream cheese, soup, and horseradish until well blended. Spread a thick layer of this mixture on each slice of roast beef. Roll up widthwise. Chill in refrigerator 1–2 hours, or until cream cheese mixture is firm. Remove and slice into $^1/_2$-inch-thick slices. Place on a serving plate so that cut spiral side is showing. Makes about 30 bites.

SIDE DISHES

DECADENT SPINACH CASSEROLE

$1/2$ medium **onion,** chopped
1 tablespoon **olive oil**
1 can (10.5 ounces) **cream of celery soup,** condensed
1 square (3 ounces) **cream cheese,** softened
2 packages (10 ounces each) **chopped frozen spinach,**
thawed and drained
$1/3$ cup **real crumbled bacon bits**
or pieces*
$1/2$ cup **crushed seasoned croutons**

Preheat oven to 350 degrees.

Saute onion in olive oil. Stir soup and cream cheese into onion until cream cheese melts. Stir in spinach and bacon. Pour into a greased 1- to $1^1/2$-quart casserole dish. Sprinkle croutons over top. Bake 35–40 minutes, or until bubbly. Makes 6 servings.

*4–5 slices bacon can be cooked and crumbled instead of using bacon bits.

FRENCH ONION MUSHROOM RICE

I cup **uncooked long-grain rice**
$^1/_4$ cup **butter,** melted
I can (10.5 ounces) **French onion soup,** condensed
I can (10.5 ounces) **beef broth**
I teaspoon **minced garlic**
I can (4 ounces) **sliced mushrooms,** drained

Preheat oven to 350 degrees.

In a bowl, combine rice and butter. Stir in soup, broth, garlic, and mushrooms. Spread rice mixture into a greased 8 x 8-inch pan. Cover with foil and then bake 60 minutes. Makes 4 servings.

SQUASH CORNBREAD CASSEROLE

I box (8.5 ounces) **corn muffin mix**

$^1/_4$ cup **butter**

2 to 3 **medium yellow summer squash,** peeled and cubed

I can (10.5 ounces) **cream of chicken soup,** condensed

I cup **sour cream**

I tablespoon **sugar**

I **green bell pepper,** chopped

I **medium onion,** chopped

salt and pepper, to taste

Bake cornbread in a greased 8 x 8-inch pan according to directions. Preheat oven to 375 degrees. Boil squash in water until tender; drain.

In a large bowl, combine cooked squash and remaining ingredients. Crumble cornbread and stir it into squash mixture. Place mixture in a 2-quart casserole dish. Bake about 35–40 minutes, or until golden brown. Makes 6 servings.

MIDWEST VEGGIE CASSEROLE

1 can (11 ounces) **white shoepeg corn,** drained
1 can (14.5 ounces) **French-cut green beans,** drained
1 can (5 ounces) **water chestnuts,** drained and chopped
$1/2$ **medium onion,** chopped
1 can (10.5 ounces) **cream of celery soup,** condensed
1 cup **sour cream**
1 cup **grated cheddar cheese**
35 **round snack crackers,** crushed

Preheat oven to 350 degrees.

In a greased 9 x 9-inch pan, layer corn, green beans, water chestnuts, and onion.

In a bowl, combine soup and sour cream. Spread mixture over layered vegetables. Sprinkle cheese and then crackers over top. Bake 30–35 minutes, or until bubbly. Makes 6–8 servings.

EASY CAULIFLOWER CASSEROLE

1 **head cauliflower,** washed and cut into florets
1 can (10.5 ounces) **cream of chicken soup,** condensed*
1/3 cup **mayonnaise**
1 teaspoon **Worcestershire sauce**
1 cup **grated cheddar cheese**
1/2 cup **crushed seasoned croutons**

Preheat oven to 350 degrees.

In a saucepan, boil cauliflower until tender. Drain and place in a greased 2-quart casserole dish. Stir in soup, mayonnaise, Worcestershire, and cheese. Sprinkle croutons over top and then bake 30 minutes. Makes 6 servings.

*Condensed cheddar cheese soup can be substituted.

GRILLED POTATOES, MUSHROOMS AND ONION

6	**medium potatoes,** thinly sliced
	salt and pepper, to taste
I can (10.5 ounces)	**cream of mushroom soup,** condensed
I package (6 ounces)	**sliced fresh mushrooms**
I	**medium onion,** thinly sliced
$^1/_4$ cup	**butter,** cut into small cubes
2 teaspoons	**Italian seasoning**
I teaspoon	**minced garlic**

Preheat an outdoor grill.

Place a large, heavy duty aluminum foil strip, big enough to hold all the ingredients, shiny side up on the counter. Lightly spray foil with vegetable oil. Place potatoes evenly over the center of the foil, leaving room around all the edges. Salt and pepper to taste. Spread soup over potatoes. Layer mushrooms and onion over soup layer. Place butter over and around the vegetables. Sprinkle seasonings over top. Fold foil over or top with another layer of aluminum foil. Seal edges by folding. Grill over medium heat on top rack for 50–60 minutes or until vegetables are tender. Makes 6–8 servings.

VEGETABLE CUSTARD CUPS

1 can (10.75 ounces)	**cream of celery soup,** condensed
3	**large eggs**
1/4 teaspoon	**nutmeg**
1/2 teaspoon	**white pepper**
2 cups	**finely diced lightly steamed vegetables***
2 cups	**grated Monterey Jack cheese**
2 tablespoons	**grated Parmesan cheese**

Preheat oven to 350 degrees.

Process all ingredients in a food processor or blender. Pour mixture into six 1-cup custard baking cups that have been sprayed with nonstick cooking spray. Set cups in a 9 x 13-inch baking pan and fill pan with hot water until level is halfway up the sides of the cups. Bake 40–45 minutes, or until set in center and lightly brown on top. Let sit 5 minutes before serving. Makes 6 servings.

*Try using any combination of broccoli, cauliflower, spinach, mushrooms, squash, and onions.

SOUPER SCALLOPED POTATOES

1/2 cup	**thinly sliced celery**
1/2 cup	**diced onion**
2 cans (10.75 ounces each)	**cheddar cheese soup,** condensed
1 can (12 ounces)	**evaporated milk**
8 cups	**peeled and thinly sliced russet potatoes**
1 cup	**grated cheddar cheese**

Preheat oven to 350 degrees.

In a bowl, mix together celery, onion, soup, and evaporated milk. Layer in a 9 x 13-inch pan in the following order: half the soup mixture, half the potato slices and half the cheese; repeat layers. Cover with foil and bake 50 minutes. Uncover and bake another 20–30 minutes, or until cooked through, bubbly, and golden brown on top. Makes 6–8 servings as a side dish.

CELERY VARIATION: Replace soup with cream of celery soup. Mix 1 teaspoon celery salt into soup. Replace cheddar cheese with Swiss or Havarti cheese.

SOUTHWEST VARIATION: Replace soup with southwest pepper jack soup. Replace celery with 1 can (4 ounces) diced mild green chiles. Replace cheddar cheese with pepper jack cheese.

WORLD'S BEST BAKED BEANS

4 strips	**bacon,** diced
1	**yellow onion,** diced
1 each	**green and red bell pepper,** diced
1 can (10.75 ounces)	**tomato soup,** condensed
2 tablespoons	**mustard**
1 teaspoon	**liquid smoke**
$^1/_4$ cup	**brown sugar**
1 can (16 ounces)	**white beans,** drained
1 can (16 ounces)	**pinto beans,** drained
2 cans (16 ounces each)	**baked beans,** with liquid

Preheat oven to 350 degrees.

In a frying pan, cook bacon pieces over medium-high heat until crisp. Add onion and bell peppers and cook another 2–3 minutes, or until limp. Drain oil and then transfer mixture to a 3- to 4-quart casserole dish. Add remaining ingredients and mix well. Bake about 1 hour, or until cooked in center and bubbly around edges. Makes 10–12 servings.

CAESAR VEGGIE BAKE

2 bags (16 ounces each) **frozen broccoli, carrots, and cauliflower**
1 can (10.75 ounces) **cream of celery soup,** condensed
1 can (10.75 ounces) **cream of onion soup,** condensed
1 container (8 ounces) **garlic-and-herb flavored cream cheese,** softened
$1/2$ cup **grated Parmesan cheese**
1 bag (6 ounces) **garlic or Caesar flavored croutons,** crushed

Preheat oven to 350 degrees.

Cook veggies until just tender according to package directions.

In a large bowl, stir together soups, cream cheese, and Parmesan cheese and then mix with cooked vegetables. Spread in a 2-quart casserole dish and sprinkle croutons over top. Bake 25–30 minutes, or until browned and bubbling. Makes 6–8 servings as a side dish.

CHEESY BAKED
CORN PUDDING

1 can (10.75 ounces)	**cream of celery soup,** condensed
$^1/_2$ cup	**milk**
$^1/_2$ cup	**sour cream**
3	**large eggs**
2 cups	**fresh or thawed frozen corn**
$^1/_2$ cup	**cornmeal**
1 cup	**grated white cheese***
$^1/_4$ cup	**grated Parmesan cheese**
3 tablespoons	**thinly sliced green onion**

Preheat oven to 350 degrees.

In a food processor or blender, blend soup, milk, sour cream, and eggs until smooth. Pour into an 8 x 8-inch baking pan that has been sprayed with nonstick cooking spray. Stir in corn, cornmeal, cheese, and onion. Bake 40–45 minutes, or until firm in center and lightly brown on top. Makes 4–6 servings.

*Any mild firm white cheese works well here such as mozzarella, Monterey Jack, provolone, Havarti, or Baby Swiss.

CREAMY BAKED RISOTTO PRIMAVERA

1 can (10.75 ounces)	**cream of asparagus soup,** condensed
1 1/2 cups	**water**
1 can (12 ounces)	**evaporated milk**
1/4 cup	**grated Parmesan cheese**
1 teaspoon	**salt**
1 cup	**diced asparagus**
1/2 cup	**diced bell pepper,** any color
1 cup	**uncooked risotto rice***
2 tablespoons	**dried basil or parsley flakes**

Preheat oven to 400 degrees.

In a bowl, stir together all ingredients. Pour into a 2 1/2-quart casserole dish. Cover and bake 30 minutes and then uncover and stir. Bake uncovered another 10 minutes. Remove from oven and let stand 10 minutes before serving. Garnish with additional parsley or basil flakes, if desired. Makes 6–8 servings as a side dish.

*Do not rinse risotto before using in recipe. This will destroy the starch, and risotto will not be creamy.

GARLIC MUSHROOM VARIATION: Replace asparagus soup with cream of mushroom and roasted garlic soup. Replace asparagus with diced button mushrooms. Replace bell peppers with diced yellow onion.

CLASSIC GREEN BEAN BAKE

4 cups **fresh green beans***
I can (10.75 ounces) **cream of mushroom soup,** condensed
$^1/_2$ cup **milk**
I tablespoon **soy sauce**
I can (3.5 ounces) **French fried onions,** divided

Preheat oven to 350 degrees.

Cut ends from green beans. Steam or microwave green beans to tender crisp stage, about 3 minutes. In a 2-quart casserole dish, mix soup, milk, soy sauce, beans, and half the onions. Bake 25–30 minutes, or until bubbly on sides and cooked through. Remove from oven, stir and then sprinkle remaining onions over top. Bake for another 10–12 minutes, or until onions are browned. Makes 4–6 servings.

*Frozen and thawed green beans can be substituted for a quicker version.

MEDITERRANEAN STYLE VARIATION: Omit the soy sauce and onions. Add I teaspoon Italian seasoning and $^1/_4$ cup grated Parmesan cheese. Top with sliced tomatoes and $^1/_2$ cup grated mozzarella cheese.

SOUTHWEST STYLE VARIATION: Omit soy sauce, milk, and onions. Replace soup with southwest pepper jack soup. Add $^1/_2$ cup salsa. Top with $^1/_2$ cup grated cheddar cheese and I cup crushed corn chips.

ASIAN STYLE VARIATION: Omit the onions. Add I can (4 ounces) sliced water chestnuts, chopped. Top with I cup crunchy chow mein noodles.

Soups & Stews

SIZZLING RICE SOUP

2 cups	**cooked white rice**
2 cans (26 ounces each)	**chicken and rice soup,** condensed
8 cups	**water**
$^1/_2$ pound	**cooked deli tiny cocktail shrimp**
1 cup	**thinly sliced green onions**
1 can (8 ounces)	**sliced water chestnuts,** drained and chopped
1 cup	**frozen peas or frozen pea pods,** chopped
2 cups	**thinly sliced celery**
$^1/_4$ cup	**soy sauce**
2 tablespoons	**peanut oil**

Preheat oven to 300 degrees.

Spread rice onto a large jellyroll pan sprayed with nonstick cooking spray. Bake 60 minutes, stirring occasionally to break up any clumps. About 10 minutes before rice is done baking, place all remaining ingredients except peanut oil in a large stockpot. Bring to a boil and then simmer for 10 minutes. Ladle soup into serving bowls and place on table.

In a large frying pan or wok, heat peanut oil. Remove rice from oven and immediately cook in wok for 3–5 minutes over medium-high heat, stirring constantly until rice is lightly brown and puffed. Add about $^1/_4$ cup rice to each serving bowl. Enjoy the sizzle—it will only last a few seconds, but will be a show-stopper! Makes 8 servings.

DINNER STEW IN A PUMPKIN

1	**medium whole pumpkin,** about 8 to 10 pounds
3	**large potatoes,** peeled
1	**yellow onion**
4 stalks	**celery**
3	**carrots,** peeled
3	**boneless, skinless chicken breasts,** cooked
2 tablespoons	**butter**
1 can (26 ounces)	**cream of chicken soup,** condensed
8 ounces	**sliced mushrooms**
1 tablespoon	**garlic powder**
1 tablespoon	**seasoned salt**
1 tablespoon	**Worcestershire sauce**

Preheat oven to 350 degrees.

Cut the top off the pumpkin so that the lid can still sit on top. Clean out the seeds and slime; place pumpkin on a baking sheet. Dice all vegetables and chicken to uniform sized $1/2$-inch cubes.

In a large frying pan, cook potatoes in butter about 3 minutes over medium-high heat. Stir in onion, celery, and carrots and cook another 5 minutes, stirring occasionally, until all vegetables are cooked through to firm stage. Mix in chicken, soup, mushrooms, garlic powder, salt, and Worcestershire sauce. Pour this mixture into pumpkin and place top back on pumpkin. Place in oven on lowest rack and bake 1 hour. Remove top and bake another 20–30 minutes, or until mixture inside is bubbling. Place whole pumpkin on as a centerpiece. Serve in large flat bowls. When serving, scoop out some of the pumpkin meat with the stew mixture. Makes 8–10 servings.

WEDDING SOUP

I pound	**ground turkey**
2	**large eggs**
$^1/_4$ cup	**seasoned breadcrumbs**
$^1/_4$ cup	**grated Parmesan cheese**
2 cans (26 ounces each)	**chicken and rice soup,** condensed
6 cups	**water**
I box (10 ounces)	**frozen chopped spinach**

In a medium mixing bowl, mix together turkey, eggs, breadcrumbs, and cheese. Form mixture into small balls the size of marbles.

In a large pot, bring soup, water, and spinach to a boil. Meanwhile, saute meatballs in a frying pan sprayed with nonstick cooking spray, stirring often until well browned. Add browned meatballs to soup mixture and simmer for about 5 minutes. Serve hot with additional cheese sprinkled on top as a garnish, if desired. Makes 8–10 servings.

CHICKEN ENCHILADA SOUP

¹/₂ cup	**thinly sliced green onion**
I cup	**cooked diced chicken**
2 tablespoons	**butter**
I can (10.75 ounces)	**chicken chile verde soup,** condensed
I can (20 ounces)	**red enchilada sauce**
I can (14 ounces)	**chicken broth**
I teaspoon	**chili powder**
I teaspoon	**cumin**
I cup	**sour cream**
I cup	**grated cheddar cheese**
4	**corn tortillas**

Saute onion and chicken in butter in a large saucepan over medium-high heat until onion is limp and chicken is lightly browned. Stir in soup, enchilada sauce, broth, and spices. Bring to a simmer. Stir in sour cream and cheese. Simmer a few minutes more until cheese is melted. Remove from heat. Cut tortillas into very thin, matchstick size strips. Stir tortilla strips into soup just before serving. Makes 4–6 servings.

CREAMY CORN CHOWDER

2 tablespoons	**butter**
$^1/_2$ cup	**thinly sliced green onion**
$^1/_2$ cup	**diced cooked ham**
2 cups	**fresh or thawed frozen corn**
2 cans (10.75 ounces each)	**cream of potato soup,** condensed
2 cups	**milk**
$^1/_2$ teaspoon	**pepper**
$^1/_2$ cup	**sour cream**

Heat butter in a large soup pot over medium-high heat. Add onion and saute until limp, about 2 minutes, stirring frequently. Add remaining ingredients except sour cream and simmer for 15–20 minutes, stirring occasionally. Remove from heat and stir in sour cream; serve warm. Makes 6–8 servings.

AUTUMN MUSHROOM SOUP

6 ounces	**sliced fresh mushrooms**
$^1/_2$ tablespoon	**minced garlic**
$^1/_4$ cup	**butter or margarine**
2 cans (10.75 ounces each)	**cream of mushroom soup,** condensed
1 cup	**half-and-half**
1 cup	**milk**
1 teaspoon	**dried rosemary,** crushed
$^1/_2$ teaspoon	**paprika**

In a 2-quart saucepan, saute mushrooms and garlic in butter until tender. Stir in soup, half-and-half, milk, rosemary, and paprika. Cook over medium-low heat without boiling until hot. Serve in bread bowls. Makes 4 servings.

CREAMY VARIATION: Before serving, blend soup in batches in a blender or food processor.

BACON RED POTATO CHOWDER

8 slices	**bacon,** cut into 1-inch pieces
2 cups	**cubed new red potatoes**
$^1/_2$	**medium onion,** chopped
1 cup	**sour cream**
1 $^1/_4$ cups	**milk**
1 can (10.5 ounces)	**cream of chicken soup,** condensed
1 can (11 ounces)	**Green Giant Mexicorn,** drained
$^1/_2$ teaspoon	**pepper**
$^1/_2$ teaspoon	**crushed thyme**

In a 3-quart saucepan, cook bacon over medium heat for 5 minutes; add potatoes and onion. Continue cooking, stirring occasionally, until potatoes are tender, about 15–20 minutes. Add remaining ingredients. Reduce heat to medium-low and continue cooking, stirring constantly, until heated through, about 10–15 minutes. Makes 6–8 servings.

EASY CLAM CHOWDER

I can (14.5 ounces) **diced potatoes,** drained
I can (10.5 ounces) **cream of celery soup,** condensed
I can (10.75 ounces) **cream of potato soup,** condensed
I can (6.5 ounces) **minced clams,** with liquid
$^1/_4$ cup **dried minced onion**
$2^1/_2$ cups **half-and-half**
I teaspoon **pepper**

In a 3-quart pan, combine all ingredients. Simmer over medium heat without boiling, stirring occasionally until hot and onions are reconstituted. Makes 6–8 servings.

CHEESY SAUSAGE SOUP

I pound	**sage-flavored ground sausage**
I	**small onion,** diced
I package (8.8 ounces)	**precooked ready long-grain and wild rice**
2 cans (10.75 ounces each)	**cream of potato soup,** condensed
I¹/₄ cups	**milk**
I can (12 ounces)	**evaporated milk**
2 cups	**grated cheddar cheese**

In a frying pan, brown sausage and onion together until meat is crumbly and cooked; drain if necessary.

In a 4-quart pot, combine sausage and onion with rice, soup, milk, and evaporated milk. Cook over medium heat until warm. Slowly stir in cheese and continue to cook over medium heat until cheese is melted. Makes 6–8 servings.

PORK STEW

1 1/2 pounds **pork stew meat,** cubed*
2 cans (10.75 ounces each) **golden mushroom soup,** condensed
1 **medium onion,** chopped
25 **baby carrots,** cut into thirds
6 ounces **sliced fresh mushrooms**

In a greased 4- to 5 1/2-quart slow cooker, combine all ingredients. Cover and cook on high heat for 3–4 hours or on low heat for 6–8 hours. Makes 8–10 servings.

*Venison or beef stew meat can be used in place of pork.

OYSTER AND SHRIMP SOUP

I can (10.75 ounces) **cream of shrimp soup,** condensed
I can (10.5 ounces) **cream of potato soup,** condensed
I can (10.75 ounces) **oyster stew,** condensed
I cup **small shrimp,** cooked and peeled
2 cups **half-and-half**
$^1/_2$ cup **milk**
I teaspoon **thyme or rosemary**
$^1/_2$ teaspoon **pepper**

Combine all ingredients in a 3- to 4-quart saucepan. Stirring constantly, simmer over medium heat for 20 minutes until heated through. Serve with French bread and oyster crackers. Makes 6–8 servings.

TACO STEW

1 pound	**ground beef,** browned and drained
1 envelope	**taco seasoning**
1 can (10.75 ounces)	**tomato soup,** condensed
1 can (15.25 ounces)	**black beans,** rinsed and drained
4 cups	**water**
$^1/_2$	**medium onion,** chopped
4	**carrots,** chopped
3	**potatoes,** peeled and cubed
1 can (15.25 ounces)	**kernel corn,** with liquid

Combine all ingredients in a 4- to 6-quart pot. Bring to a boil. Reduce heat and simmer an additional 35–45 minutes, or until vegetables are done. Makes 6–8 servings.

POULTRY & SEAFOOD

WEEKNIGHT BISTRO CHICKEN

4	**boneless, skinless chicken breasts**
3 tablespoons	**peanut or canola oil**
I can (I4 ounces)	**diced tomatoes,** undrained
I can (I0.75 ounces)	**French onion soup,** condensed
I can (I0.75 ounces)	**golden mushroom soup,** condensed
2 tablespoons	**minced garlic**
2 cups	**grated Swiss or Havarti cheese**
8 cups	**cooked rice or egg noodles**

Lay chicken breasts flat on a cutting board. With a large flat knife parallel to the cutting surface, cut each chicken breast in half, forming two large flat planks. Saute chicken planks in batches in a large frying pan in oil over medium-high heat until browned, about 2 minutes on each side. Place browned chicken in a 4- to 6-quart slow cooker.

In a bowl, mix together remaining ingredients except cheese and noodles and pour into slow cooker, moving chicken planks so that sauce is evenly distributed throughout. Cook on high heat for 3–4 hours or low heat for 6–8 hours. Remove chicken to an ovenproof serving platter. Sprinkle with cheese. Broil in oven for 2–3 minutes, or until cheese is bubbling and lightly browned. Mash sauce with a potato masher until there are no large chunks. Use sauce to top rice or noodles. Makes 4–6 servings.

CHICKEN DURANGO

3 tablespoons **butter**

3 **boneless, skinless chicken breasts**

1 **large yellow onion,** julienned

1 **green bell pepper,** julienned

1 **red bell pepper,** julienned

1 can (10.75 ounces) **chicken chile verde soup,** condensed*

$^1/_2$ cup **water**

$^1/_2$ cup **sour cream**

8 cups **hot cooked regular or Spanish rice**

Heat butter in a large frying pan or wok. Thinly slice chicken breasts and saute over medium-high heat until chicken turns white. Add onion and bell peppers and cook until onion is translucent, about 3 minutes.

In a bowl, mix together soup, water, and sour cream. Pour into pan and simmer about 2 minutes. Serve over rice with the chicken mixture. Makes 6–8 servings.

*Cream of chicken soup can be substituted.

SOUTHWEST CHICKEN POLENTA STACKS

3	**boneless, skinless chicken breasts,** diced
2 tablespoons	**canola oil**
1	**green bell pepper,** diced
1	**large onion,** diced
2 cans (10.75 ounces each)	**southwest pepper jack soup,** condensed
2 tubes (18 ounces each)	**ready-to-eat polenta**
4 cups	**grated pepper jack cheese**
1	**red bell pepper, diced**

In a medium frying pan, saute chicken in oil over medium-high heat until lightly browned. Add green bell pepper and onion. Saute for 2–3 minutes, or until onion is limp. Stir in soup and reduce heat to low. Slice polenta into $1/2$-inch-thick slices and arrange on a large serving platter. Microwave 2 minutes until heated through. Spoon chicken mixture onto polenta slices. Sprinkle cheese and then red bell pepper on top. Serve warm, two or three stacks per person. Makes 6–8 servings.

CHILE VERDE
CHICKEN ENCHILADAS

18	**corn tortillas**
3 tablespoons	**butter**
1	**rotisserie chicken,** about 4 to 5 pounds
1 can (14 ounces)	**green or red enchilada sauce**
1 can (10.75 ounces)	**chicken chile verde soup,** condensed*
16 ounces	**Monterey Jack cheese,** grated
1/2 cup	**thinly sliced green onion**

Preheat oven to 375 degrees.

In a frying pan, saute each tortilla over medium-high heat in a little of the butter until cooked through but not crisp, about 1 minute on each side. Remove meat from chicken and shred with two forks.

In a small mixing bowl, mix together enchilada sauce and soup. Pour 1 cup of sauce in the bottom of a 9 x 13-inch pan. Roll about 1/3 cup cheese, 1/4 cup shredded chicken, and 1 teaspoon green onion in each tortilla. Place each roll in pan, seam side down. Pour remaining sauce over top of rolls and sprinkle remaining cheese on top. Bake 25–30 minutes, or until cooked through and bubbling. Makes 8 servings.

*Cream of chicken soup can be substituted.

CHEESE ENCHILADA VARIATION: Instead of chicken use a total of 32 ounces Monterey Jack cheese, grated. Replace soup with southwest pepper jack cheese soup.

CHICKEN AND BROCCOLI CUPS

3	**boneless, skinless chicken breasts,** cooked and diced
I can (10.75 ounces)	**broccoli cheddar soup,** condensed
2 cups	**chopped, lightly steamed broccoli**
I	**carrot,** peeled and grated
I tablespoon	**Dijon mustard**
I teaspoon	**garlic powder**
$^1/_2$ teaspoon	**white pepper**
I box (17 ounces)	**frozen puff pastry,** thawed
$^1/_2$ cup	**grated Parmesan cheese**

Preheat oven to 350 degrees.

In a large bowl, mix together the first 7 ingredients and set aside. Lay both pastry sheets on a nonstick surface. Cut each pastry sheet into 4 squares, forming a total of 8 squares. Press the pastry squares into large muffin tins or individual ramekins that have been sprayed with nonstick cooking spray. Fill each pastry cup with chicken mixture. Bake 25–30 minutes, or until bubbly and golden brown. Remove from oven and sprinkle Parmesan cheese over each cup. Makes 8 servings.

HOT TURKEY SALAD

2 cans (10.75 ounces each)	**cream of celery soup,** condensed
1 cup	**regular or light sour cream**
2 tablespoons	**lemon juice**
1 teaspoon	**salt**
1 teaspoon	**white pepper**
6 cups	**^{1}/2-inch cubed cooked turkey**
2 cups	**finely diced celery**
^{1}/2 cup	**thinly sliced green onion**
6	**hard-boiled eggs,** divided
^{3}/4 cup	**sliced toasted almonds,** divided

Preheat oven to 350 degrees.

In a 3-quart casserole dish, stir together soup, sour cream, lemon juice, salt, and pepper. Stir in turkey, celery, and onion. Peel and slice eggs. Stir half the eggs and ^{1}/2 cup almonds into chicken mixture. Sprinkle remaining egg and almonds on top. Bake 40–50 minutes, or until cooked through and bubbly; serve warm. Makes 6–8 servings.

COMPANY'S COMING CHICKEN

2 tablespoons	**canola oil**
10	**skinless chicken thighs**
	(about 5 pounds)
2 teaspoons	**garlic powder**
2 cans (10.75 ounces each)	**golden mushroom soup,**
	condensed
2 tablespoons	**balsamic vinegar**
1 cup	**light sour cream**
2 cups	**thinly sliced button mushrooms**

Preheat oven to 350 degrees.

In a large frying pan, heat oil to medium-high heat. Saute chicken in batches for about 5 minutes on each side until well browned. Sprinkle garlic powder on cooked chicken. Mix together soup, vinegar, and sour cream. Spread $1/2$ cup on bottom of a 9 x 13-inch pan. Place chicken in pan, completely filling pan. Sprinkle mushrooms evenly on top. Spread remaining soup mixture over top, completely covering top and sealing edges. Bake 60–70 minutes, or until well browned on top. Serve using excess sauce over cooked rice, noodles or diced red potatoes, if desired. Makes 4–6 servings.

CHICKEN CURRY IN A HURRY

2 pounds	**chicken breasts** (about 4 breasts)
4 tablespoons	**extra virgin olive oil,** divided
1	**medium yellow onion,** diced
2 cans (10.75 ounces each)	**cream of celery soup,** condensed
1 can (14 ounces)	**coconut milk,** shaken
1 tablespoon	**mild curry powder or curry paste**
1 teaspoon	**ginger**
1 teaspoon	**garlic powder**
1 teaspoon	**salt**
1 cup	**frozen tiny peas**
$1/2$ cup	**roasted cashews,** diced
8 cups	**cooked rice**

Slice chicken into $1/4$-inch-thick slices, each about an inch long. Heat 2 tablespoons oil in a wok or large frying pan. Saute chicken over medium-high heat until lightly browned, about 8–10 minutes. Remove chicken and add remaining oil and onion, sauteing about 3 minutes or until onion is translucent.

In a bowl, mix together soup, coconut milk, curry, and spices. Add soup mixture to wok and bring to a simmer, stirring constantly. Stir chicken back in and then add peas and cashews; turn off heat. Serve over rice. Makes 6–8 servings.

CREAMY ITALIAN CHICKEN

4 **boneless, skinless chicken breasts**
1 envelope **Italian salad dressing mix**
$^1/_4$ cup **water**
1 package (8 ounces) **cream cheese,** softened
1 can (10.75 ounces) **cream of chicken soup,** condensed

Preheat oven to 350 degrees.

Place chicken breasts on the bottom of a greased 9 x 13-inch pan. Combine salad dressing mix and water; spread evenly over chicken. Combine cream cheese and soup; spread evenly over chicken. Cover pan with foil and then bake 40 minutes. Makes 4 servings.

CHICKEN FETTUCCINE

2	**boneless, skinless chicken breasts,** cubed
1 tablespoon	**minced garlic**
$1/2$	**medium onion,** chopped
2 tablespoons	**olive oil**
2 teaspoons	**Italian seasoning**
1 can (10.5 ounces)	**cream of mushroom soup,** condensed
$1/2$ cup	**milk**
$1/2$ cup	**grated Parmesan cheese**
1 bag (16 ounces)	**fettuccine pasta**

In a large frying pan, saute chicken, garlic, and onion in hot oil until chicken is no longer pink. Sprinkle seasoning over chicken. Stir in soup, milk, and cheese. Simmer over low heat 10–15 minutes. While sauce simmers, cook pasta according to package directions and drain. Serve sauce over hot cooked pasta. Makes 3–4 servings.

PARMESAN CHICKEN AND RICE BAKE

1 pound	**boneless, skinless chicken breasts,** cut into small pieces
1 tablespoon	**olive oil**
	salt and pepper, to taste
1 can (10.5 ounces)	**cream of chicken soup,** condensed
1$2/3$ cups	**milk**
$1/2$ cup	**grated Parmesan cheese**
$1/2$ teaspoon	**Italian seasoning**
1	**large tomato,** diced
2 cups	**uncooked instant rice**

In a frying pan, saute chicken in hot oil until lightly browned. Season with salt and pepper. While chicken cooks, combine soup, milk, cheese, and seasoning in a 2-quart saucepan. Heat until it starts to bubble. Stir in tomato and instant rice. Cover and cook over low heat for 5 minutes, or until rice is done. Serve chicken over individual servings of rice. Makes 4 servings.

CREAMY CHICKEN SPAGHETTI

I can (28 ounces)	**diced tomatoes seasoned with basil, garlic, and oregano,** with liquid
I	**medium onion,** chopped
¹/₂ teaspoon	**minced garlic**
I bag (16 ounces)	**spaghetti**
I can (10.5 ounces)	**cream of chicken soup,** condensed
I cans (12.5 ounces)	**white chicken,** with broth
I tablespoon	**Worcestershire sauce**
I can (10.5 ounces)	**cream of mushroom soup,** condensed
I cup	**grated medium cheddar cheese**

Preheat oven to 350 degrees. In a 2¹/₂- to 3-quart saucepan, combine tomatoes, onion, and garlic. Simmer over medium heat until onion is tender.

Cook spaghetti according to package directions. Stir cream of chicken soup, chicken, and Worcestershire sauce into tomato mixture. Simmer over low heat until spaghetti is done. Drain spaghetti and place in a greased 9 x 13-inch pan. Spoon hot chicken mixture over spaghetti noodles. Spread cream of mushroom soup over top. Sprinkle cheese over soup. Bake 15–20 minutes, or until bubbly. Makes 6–8 servings.

CORNBREAD CHICKEN

I (2.25-pound)	**lemon pepper rotisserie cooked whole chicken**
I bag (16 ounces)	**frozen mixed vegetables,** thawed and drained
I can (10.5 ounces)	**cream of chicken soup,** condensed
I can (10.5 ounces)	**cream of celery soup,** condensed
1/2 teaspoon	**black pepper**
I box (8.5 ounces)	**corn muffin mix**

Preheat oven to 350 degrees. Shred cooked chicken meat.

In a bowl, combine chicken, vegetables, soups, and pepper. Spread chicken mixture into a greased 9 x 13-inch pan. Prepare muffin mix batter according to package directions. Pour batter evenly over chicken layer. Bake 30–35 minutes, or until golden brown and bubbly. Makes 6–8 servings.

CHICKEN CORDON BLEU BAKE

5 to 6 **boneless, skinless chicken breasts,** cubed
1 can (10.5 ounces) **cream of celery soup,** condensed
1 can (10.5 ounces) **cream of chicken soup,** condensed
$^1/_2$ pound **cubed ham steak**
8 ounces **Swiss cheese,** grated

Preheat oven to 375 degrees.

Place raw cubed chicken in a greased 9 x 13-inch pan. Spread soups over chicken. Layer ham and cheese over soup. Bake 40–50 minutes, or until chicken is done. Makes 6–8 servings.

CAJUN JAMBALAYA

1/2 each	**red and green bell peppers,** diced
I box (8 ounces)	**frozen sliced okra**
2 cups	**uncooked rice**
I can (10.75 ounces)	**French onion soup,** condensed
3 cups	**water**
I teaspoon	**salt,** or more to taste
1/4 cup	**Louisiana-style cayenne pepper hot sauce** (optional)
I cup	**cooked chopped sausage, bacon, or ham**
1/2 pound	**cooked cocktail shrimp**
I box (10 ounces)	**frozen peas**

Combine bell peppers, okra, rice, soup, water, salt, and hot sauce in a wok or large frying pan. Cover and simmer 20–25 minutes, or until all liquid is absorbed and rice is cooked. Add meat, shrimp, and peas; heat through and serve hot. Makes 6–8 servings.

SEAFOOD GUMBO CASSEROLE

2 cans (10.75 ounces each) **chicken gumbo soup,** condensed
2 cups **water**
1 teaspoon **gumbo file or Cajun seasoning**
1 teaspoon **garlic powder**
1 bag (16 ounces) **frozen okra, onions, and tomatoes**
1 cup **uncooked rice**
$^1/_2$ cup **diced ham**
1 bag (16 ounces) **frozen cooked cocktail shrimp**

Preheat oven to 350 degrees.

Stir together all ingredients in a $2^1/_2$- to 3-quart casserole dish. Bake 60 minutes. Remove from oven and stir before serving to fluff rice. Makes 6–8 servings.

MARYLAND CRAB CAKES

1 can (10.75 ounces) **cream of shrimp soup,** condensed
1 **large egg**
32 ounces **fresh crabmeat***
1/2 cup **minced green onion**
2 tablespoons **dried dill**
2 tablespoons **parsley**
1 teaspoon **Old Bay seasoning**
1 cup toasted **breadcrumbs**
1/4 cup **peanut oil**

In a medium mixing bowl, blend soup and egg with a fork until smooth. Stir in remaining ingredients, except oil, until blended. Make patties about 4 inches in diameter and 1 1/2 inches thick. Chill patties in refrigerator for at least 30 minutes, or overnight. Heat oil in a medium frying pan to medium heat. Saute patties, a few at a time, with pan covered for about 5 minutes on each side. Patties should be well browned. Makes 12–15 patties.

Note: If patties don't stick together well after forming, return mixture to bowl and add more breadcrumbs as needed.

*Crabmeat may be replaced with an equal amount of imitation crabmeat, but it must first be finely diced.

BEEF & PORK

SOUPER TAMALE PIE

I pound	**lean ground beef**
I bunch	**green onions,** thinly sliced (about I cup)
2 cans (I5 ounces each)	**ready-to-serve steak fajita soup**
I can (6 ounces)	**tomato paste**
2 cups	**frozen corn,** thawed
I can (4 ounces)	**sliced black olives**
I tablespoon	**chipotle chili powder,** or more to taste
3 cups	**grated cheddar cheese,** divided
I	**large egg,** lightly beaten with a fork
I cup	**milk**
2 tablespoons	**canola oil**
$^3/_4$ cup	**cornmeal**
$^3/_4$ cup	**flour**
I tablespoon	**baking powder**

Preheat oven to 400 degrees.

In a frying pan, brown the ground beef; drain oil and place in a 3- to 4-quart casserole dish. Stir onions, soup, tomato paste, corn, olives, chili powder, and 2$^1/_2$ cups cheese into the cooked beef.

In a medium mixing bowl, stir egg, milk, and oil together. Mix dry ingredients together and stir into egg mixture. Pour on top of mixture in casserole. Bake 20–25 minutes, or until cornbread topping is cooked through in the middle and lightly browned on top. Remove from oven and sprinkle remaining cheese on top; serve warm. Makes 8–10 servings.

VARIATION: Replace ground beef with ground turkey or chicken. Replace soup with chicken fajita or chicken tortilla soup.

BROCCOLI BEEF STIR-FRY

16 ounces	**top round or sirloin steak**
1 tablespoon	**minced garlic**
1 tablespoon	**ginger**
4 tablespoons	**cornstarch,** divided
2 tablespoons	**soy sauce**
2 tablespoons	**peanut oil**
4 cups	**diced fresh broccoli**
$^1/_2$	**red bell pepper,** sliced in thin strips
1 can (10.75 ounces)	**French onion soup,** condensed
8 cups	**hot cooked rice**

Slice beef in very thin strips and place in a small mixing bowl. Stir garlic, ginger, 2 tablespoons cornstarch, and soy sauce into beef. Let sit on counter at room temperature for 20 minutes to marinate. Heat oil in a large frying pan or wok. Saute beef for about 2 minutes, stirring occasionally. Add broccoli and bell pepper and cook another 2 minutes, stirring occasionally. Drain a little of the broth from the soup into a small bowl and mix remaining cornstarch into broth. Add cornstarch mixture and remainder of soup to pan. Stir and cook another 3–5 minutes, or until sauce has thickened slightly. Serve immediately over hot rice. Makes 6–8 servings.

UNSTUFFED CABBAGE

1 **small cabbage,** shredded
2 pounds **lean ground beef**
1 **large yellow onion,** diced
1 tablespoon **minced garlic**
2 teaspoons **seasoned salt**
1 can (26 ounces) **tomato soup,** condensed
1 tablespoon **Worcestershire sauce**
2 tablespoons **brown sugar**
2 cups **cooked rice**

Preheat oven to 375 degrees.

In a large stockpot, bring about 2 quarts water to a boil. Turn off heat and add cabbage. Let stand 10 minutes to soften and then drain.

In a large frying pan or wok, cook the ground beef over medium-high heat until it is no longer pink, about 5 minutes, stirring frequently to break up clumps. Add onion, garlic, and salt to beef. Cook another 2–3 minutes, or until onion is limp. Stir in soup, Worcestershire sauce, and brown sugar.

In a 4-quart casserole dish, layer one-third of the cabbage, 1 cup rice, and half of the meat mixture; repeat layers and top with remaining cabbage. Cover and bake 45 minutes. Uncover and bake another 15 minutes. Makes 8–10 servings.

CORN CHIP CASSEROLE

1 pound	**ground beef**
1 can (10 ounces)	**tomatoes and green chiles,** with liquid
1 can (10.5 ounces)	**cream of mushroom soup,** condensed
1 can (15 ounces)	**black beans,** rinsed and drained
3 1/2 to 4 cups	**Fritos corn chips**
1 3/4 cups	**grated cheddar cheese**

Preheat oven to 350 degrees.

In a frying pan, brown ground beef until no longer pink; drain if necessary. Stir in tomatoes, soup, and beans. Simmer over low heat for 10 minutes. Lay chips in bottom of a 9 x 13-inch pan. Spoon beef mixture over chips and bake 15–20 minutes. Sprinkle cheese over top and bake 5 minutes more. Makes 6–8 servings.

EFFORTLESS BEEF AND MUSHROOMS

2 pounds **stew meat**
2 cans (10.5 ounces each) **cream of mushroom soup,** condensed
$^1/_2$ cup **ginger ale**
1 envelope **dry onion soup mix**
1 can (4 ounces) **mushrooms,** drained

Preheat oven to 300 degrees.

Combine all ingredients in a greased 2-quart casserole dish and cover. Bake $2^1/_2$–3 hours. Serve over hot cooked rice, egg noodles, or mashed potatoes. Makes 4–6 servings.

TATER TOT
GUMBO CASSEROLE

I pound	**ground beef**
I	**medium onion,** chopped
I bag (16 ounces)	**frozen green beans,** thawed
I can (10.75 ounces)	**chicken gumbo soup,** condensed
I can (10.5 ounces)	**chicken rice soup,** condensed
I can (10.5 ounces)	**cream of mushroom soup,** condensed
I bag (32 ounces)	**tater tots**

Preheat oven to 350 degrees.

In a frying pan, brown ground beef and onion over medium heat until no longer pink; drain if necessary. Spread beef mixture evenly in a greased 9 x 13-inch pan. Layer green beans over top.

In a small bowl, combine the soups and pour over green beans. Top with tater tots and bake 45–60 minutes, or until tater tots are crisp. Makes 6–8 servings.

WRAPPED-UP POT ROAST

1 (3- to 3 1/2-pound) **boneless pot roast**
1 can (10.5 ounces) **cream of mushroom soup,** condensed
1 envelope **dry onion soup mix**
1/4 cup **Worcestershire sauce**
2 teaspoons **minced garlic**

Preheat oven to 300 degrees. Place a 30-inch-long piece of foil in the bottom of a 9 x 13-inch pan. Place roast in center of foil.

In a bowl, combine soup, soup mix, Worcestershire sauce, and garlic. Spread soup mixture over roast. Fold foil over roast and seal all edges. Bake 3–3 1/2 hours, or until done in center. To make sure center is not pink, cut roast open. Makes 6–8 servings.

CREAMY TENDER CUBE STEAKS

4	**cube steaks**
$^1/_2$ teaspoon	**pepper**
I can (12 ounces)	**lemon-lime soda**
$^1/_4$ cup	**chopped onion**
2 cans (10.5 ounces each)	**cream of mushroom soup,** condensed

Preheat oven to 325 degrees.

Place steaks on bottom of a greased 9 x 13-inch pan. Sprinkle pepper over steaks. Pour soda over top and then sprinkle steaks with onion. Spread soup over the top. Bake I hour, or until done. Makes 4 servings.

MAIN DISH BREAD PUDDING

16 ounces	**mild Italian sausage**
1 bunch	**green onions,** sliced (about 1 cup)
2 cloves	**fresh garlic,** minced
8 cups	**day-old white bread cubes**
1 cup	**grated provolone or Monterey Jack cheese**
6	**large eggs**
3 cups	**milk**
1 can (10.75 ounces)	**cream of mushroom soup,** condensed

Preheat oven to 350 degrees.

Remove casings from sausages and crumble into a large frying pan. Cook about 3 minutes. Remove sausage and drain pan, leaving about 2 tablespoons of oil. Add onions and garlic to the pan and cook another 2 minutes. Spray a 3^1/$_2$- to 4-quart casserole dish with nonstick cooking spray. Spread half the bread cubes in the bottom. Sprinkle meat mixture and cheese evenly over top. Spread remaining bread cubes over meat.

In a bowl, mix together eggs, milk, and soup. Pour over top, making sure each bread cube is saturated. Bake 40–50 minutes, or until set in the middle and bubbling on edges. Let stand 10 minutes before serving. Makes 6–8 servings.

Southwest Bread Pudding Variation: Replace sausage with 2 boneless, skinless chicken breasts, diced. Replace garlic with 3 tablespoons minced jalapenos or green chiles. Replace soup with southwest pepper jack soup.

Garden Vegetable Variation: Replace sausage with 2 cups diced fresh vegetables. Replace soup with cream of asparagus soup.

SAUCY PORK CHOPS

4	**sirloin pork chops**
1 tablespoon	**olive oil**
$^1/_2$ bag (16 ounces)	**medium egg noodles**
1 can (10.5 ounces)	**cream of celery soup,** condensed
$^1/_2$ cup	**apple juice**
2 tablespoons	**spicy mustard**
1 tablespoon	**honey**
$^1/_2$ teaspoon	**pepper**

In a frying pan, brown pork chops in oil. Cook noodles according to package directions. While noodles cook, combine soup, juice, mustard, honey, and pepper. Pour mixture over pork chops and bring to a boil. Cover and simmer over medium heat for 5 minutes. Serve pork chops over hot cooked noodles. Makes 4 servings.

PORK CHOPS AND POTATOES

2 cans (10.5 ounces each) **cream of mushroom soup,** condensed*

1 cup **milk**

4 **potatoes,** peeled and thinly sliced

$^1/_2$ **medium onion,** chopped

salt and pepper, to taste

1$^1/_2$ teaspoons **Italian seasoning**

6 to 7 **boneless thin-cut pork chops**

Preheat oven to 400 degrees.

In a bowl, combine soup and milk. Place potatoes evenly on bottom of a greased 9 x 13-inch pan. Sprinkle onion evenly over potatoes. Season with salt and pepper. Sprinkle Italian seasoning over vegetables. Lay pork chops over vegetables. Pour soup mixture over top. Bake, covered, 50 minutes. Uncover and bake 10 minutes more, or until potatoes are tender. Makes 6–7 servings.

*Condensed cream of celery soup can be substituted.

SHREDDED BARBECUE PORK SANDWICHES

3 1/2- to 4-pound **boneless pork roast**
I can (10.5 ounces) **French onion soup,** condensed
I cup **ketchup**
1/4 cup **cider vinegar**
1/4 cup **brown sugar**
14 to 16 **hamburger buns**

Place roast in a greased 3- to 4 1/2-quart slow cooker.

In a bowl, combine soup, ketchup, vinegar, and sugar. Pour mixture over roast. Cover and cook on high heat 4–5 hours or on low heat 8–10 hours. With two forks, shred pork. Stir pork to coat with sauce. Cook for an additional 30 minutes with the lid off. Serve on hamburger buns. Makes 14–16 sandwiches.

SLOW-COOKED POTATOES AND SAUSAGE

8 cups **cubed potatoes**
1 package (16 ounces) **smoked sausage,** sliced
1 can (10.5 ounces) **cream of mushroom soup,** condensed
1 can (10.5 ounces) **vegetable beef soup,** condensed
1 teaspoon **crushed rosemary**

Combine potatoes, sausage, soups, and rosemary in a greased 5- to 6-quart slow cooker. Cover and cook on low heat for 6–8 hours. Makes 6–8 servings.

BEEF AND BEAN BURRITOS

2 pounds **ground beef**
I can (10.75 ounces) **tomato soup,** condensed
I can (16 ounces) **refried beans**
2 envelopes **taco seasoning**
$^1/_4$ cup **water**
12 **large flour tortillas**
$2^1/_2$ cups **grated cheddar cheese**

In a large frying pan, brown and crumble beef until no longer pink;
drain if necessary. Stir in soup, beans, seasoning, and water. Simmer
over low heat 5–10 minutes. Spread filling over center of warm tortillas.
Sprinkle cheese over filling and roll up burritos. Garnish with salsa,
guacamole, and sour cream if desired. Makes 12 servings.

VARIATION: Replace soup with creamy ranchero tomato soup.

NACHO VARIATION: Hot filling can also be served over tortilla chips.
Garnish with cheese, salsa, guacamole, and sour cream.

POLYNESIAN PORK AND RICE

3 pounds	**boneless pork loin or chops**
2 tablespoons	**canola oil**
I can (10.75 ounces)	**golden mushroom soup,** condensed
I tablespoon	**minced garlic**
$^{1}/_{4}$ cup	**soy sauce**
2 tablespoons	**brown sugar**
I can (20 ounces)	**pineapple chunks,** with juice
I	**red bell pepper**
I	**green bell pepper**
I	**large yellow onion**
8 cups	**hot cooked rice**

Preheat oven to 350 degrees.

Cut pork into 2-inch cubes, removing visible fat. Heat oil in a large frying pan and saute pork cubes over medium-high heat, stirring often, until well browned on all sides.

In a bowl, stir together soup, garlic, soy sauce, sugar, and pineapple juice (drained from the can of pineapple). Stir pork and sauce together and pour into a 9 x 13-inch pan. Bake I hour. Cut bell peppers and onion into I-inch chunks. Remove pork from oven and stir in vegetables. Bake another 30 minutes. Remove from oven and stir in pineapple chunks. Let stand 5 minutes before serving. Serve over hot cooked rice. Makes 6–8 servings.

Family Favorites

SPECIALTY SAUCES

For easy weeknight family meals, use one of these quick and delicious sauces to top broiled or grilled meats, or your family's favorite pasta!

Tangy Tomato Mustard Sauce:

$^1/_4$ cup **butter**
$^1/_2$ cup **sugar**
1 tablespoon **mustard**
$^1/_4$ cup **vinegar**
1 can (10.75 ounces) **tomato soup,** condensed
3 **egg yolks**

In a small saucepan over medium-high heat, melt butter and then stir in sugar until dissolved. Stir in mustard, vinegar, and soup. Heat until sauce begins to simmer. Stir in egg yolks and whisk until sauce is thickened, 3–5 minutes; serve warm. Makes 2 cups. Excellent as a sauce for roasted meats or baked ham slices.

Three Cheese Sauce:

1 can (10.75 ounces) **cheddar cheese soup,** condensed
$^2/_3$ cup **milk**
$^1/_4$ cup **grated Parmesan cheese**
$^1/_2$ cup **grated mozzarella or provolone cheese**
$^1/_2$ teaspoon **garlic powder**

Combine all ingredients in a small saucepan over medium heat and whisk until cheeses are melted and sauce is smooth. A perfect topping for steamed vegetables or pasta.

Mushroom Roasted Garlic Sauce:

      1 can (10.75 ounces) **mushroom and roasted garlic soup,** condensed

      1 cup **cream**

      5 or 6 **large button mushrooms,** finely minced

Combine soup and cream in a small saucepan over medium heat. Whisk until it begins to simmer. Stir mushrooms into saucepan and simmer a few minutes more, stirring occasionally. Great for pastas and broiled meats.

Creamy Pesto Sauce:

      1 can (10.75 ounces) **cream of potato soup,** condensed

      1 cup **cream**

      1 jar (6 ounces) **pesto**

      1 teaspoon **garlic powder**

Process soup and cream in a food processor or blender until creamy. Pour into a small saucepan and bring to a simmer over medium heat. Stir in pesto and garlic powder and simmer a few minutes more. Use for pasta or broiled fish or chicken.

Seafood Newberg Sauce:

      1 can (15 ounces) **New England clam chowder,** condensed

      1 cup **cream**

      1 package (3.5 ounces) **crabmeat**

      1 package (3.4 ounces) **shrimp,** with liquid

      2 tablespoons **grated Parmesan cheese**

Process soup and cream in a food processor or blender until creamy. Pour into a small saucepan and bring to a simmer over medium heat. Add crabmeat and shrimp. Stir in cheese. Simmer for a few minutes until well heated. Serve over broiled fish or pasta.

WINTER CHILI

2 pounds	**ground beef**
1	**medium onion,** chopped
1 envelope	**chili seasoning mix**
1/2 cup	**water**
1 can (6 ounces)	**tomato paste**
1 can (15.5 ounces)	**chili beans,** with sauce
1 can (16 ounces)	**baked beans**
1 can (10.75 ounces)	**tomato soup,** condensed
1 can (10 ounces)	**diced tomatoes with green chiles,** with liquid

In a frying pan, brown ground beef and onion together until done. Stir in chili seasoning and water. Place beef mixture in a greased 3 1/2- to 5-quart slow cooker. Stir in remaining ingredients. Cover and cook on high heat 1 1/2–2 hours or on low heat 3–4 hours. Makes 8–10 servings.

UPSIDE DOWN PIZZA CASSEROLE

2 cans (19 ounces each)	**ready-to-serve minestrone soup**
2 cans (6 ounces each)	**tomato paste**
1 teaspoon	**garlic powder**
2 teaspoons	**dry Italian seasoning**
2 cups	**diced pepperoni or cooked Italian sausage**
2 cups	**grated mozzarella cheese**
1 1/2 cups	**grated Parmesan cheese,** divided
1 tube (13 ounces)	**refrigerated pizza dough**

Preheat oven to 350 degrees.

Drain and discard 1/2 cup liquid from each of the cans of soup, and then pour remainder in a 9 x 13-inch pan. Stir in tomato paste, garlic powder, seasoning, and meat, spreading mixture evenly in pan. Sprinkle mozzarella and 1 cup Parmesan on top. Unroll pizza dough and lay on top of cheese; cut to fit. Make a few slits in dough to allow steam to escape while baking. Bake 40–50 minutes, or until crust is browned. Remove from oven and let sit 5 minutes. Cut in squares and turn upside down on each plate as you serve. Garnish with remaining cheese. Makes 8–10 servings.

CLASSIC TUNA NOODLE CASSEROLE

1 cup	**diced fresh mushrooms**
¹/₂ cup	**thinly sliced green onions**
1 tablespoon	**butter**
1 can (10.75 ounces)	**cream of mushroom soup,** condensed
¹/₂ cup	**sour cream**
1 cup	**frozen peas**
2 cans (6 ounces each)	**water-packed solid chunk tuna,** drained
1 bag (16 ounces)	**egg noodles,** cooked until just tender and drained
1 cup	**crushed potato chips**

Preheat oven to 375 degrees.

Saute mushrooms and onions in butter 2–3 minutes over medium-high heat, or until onions are limp.

In a large mixing bowl, combine soup, sour cream, peas, and tuna. Stir in mushrooms and onions. Stir in cooked noodles. Spread in a 3-quart casserole dish and sprinkle potato chips on top. Bake uncovered 25–30 minutes, or until bubbly on sides and cooked through. Makes 6–8 servings.

SOUTHWEST STYLE VARIATION: Replace soup with southwest pepper jack soup. Replace mushrooms and peas with 1 can (4 ounces) diced green chiles. Add 1 cup grated pepper jack cheese. Replace potato chips with crushed tortilla chips.

CHEESY STYLE VARIATION: Replace soup with cream of onion soup. Add 1 cup grated sharp cheddar cheese. Replace potato chips with crushed cheese puffs.

DO-IT-YOURSELF QUESADILLAS

3 cups **cooked ground turkey or beef**
3 cups **minced onion and/or peppers**
1 1/2 cups **diced fresh tomatoes**
1 can (10.75 ounces) **nacho cheese soup,** condensed
12 (8-inch) **flour tortillas**
2 cups **grated Mexican-style cheese blend**

Place meat, onion, peppers, and tomatoes in separate bowls. Allow each person to choose the amounts and types of fillings, as suggested below. Heat a 10-inch frying pan to medium heat. Spread 1 tablespoon soup on a tortilla and place it dry side down in pan. Sprinkle 1/2 cup ground meat, 1/2 cup peppers and/or onions, 1/4 cup tomatoes, and 1/3 cup cheese on top. Spread another tortilla with 1 tablespoon soup. Place soup side down on top. Press with a spatula to remove any air bubbles. Cook uncovered for about 2 minutes and then turn over and cook another 2–3 minutes. Tortillas should be golden brown and crisp on the outside. Cut into wedges with a pizza cutter. Garnish with guacamole, sour cream, and/or salsa, if desired. Makes 6 quesadillas.

VARIATION: Replace soup with chicken chile verde or southwest pepper jack soup.

SLOPPY JOES

3 pounds **ground beef**
I can (10.75 ounces) **tomato soup,** condensed
I can (10.5 ounces) **French onion soup,** condensed
$^{1}/_{2}$ cup **ketchup**
I tablespoon **mustard**
$^{1}/_{4}$ cup **packed brown sugar**
10 to 14 **hamburger buns**

In a large frying pan, brown ground beef until crumbled and no longer pink; drain if necessary. Stir in soups, ketchup, mustard, and brown sugar. Simmer over medium heat 20–30 minutes. Spoon meat mixture onto buns. Makes 10–14 sandwiches.

DEBBIE'S MUSHROOM BURGERS

I pound	**ground beef**
I can (10.5 ounces)	**cream of mushroom soup,** condensed
I can (4 ounces)	**sliced mushrooms,** drained
	salt and pepper, to taste
8	**hamburger buns**

In a frying pan, brown ground beef until no longer pink; drain if necessary. Stir in soup and mushrooms. Season with salt and pepper. Serve hot on buns. Makes 6–8 servings.

YUMMY MEATBALLS

1	**green bell pepper,** seeded and chopped
1/2	**medium onion,** chopped
1 tablespoon	**butter**
1 can (10.75 ounces)	**tomato soup,** condensed
1 can (10.5 ounces)	**chicken and rice soup,** condensed
1/2 cup	**water**
25	**frozen fully-cooked meatballs,** thawed

In a large frying pan, saute bell pepper and onion in butter until tender. Stir in soups and water. Bring to a boil. Add meatballs and return sauce to a boil. Reduce heat and simmer 15 minutes, or until meatballs are thoroughly heated. Makes 5–6 servings.

EASY CHICKEN POTPIE

2	**boneless, skinless chicken breasts,** cooked and cubed
2 cans (10.75 ounces each)	**cream of chicken soup with herbs,** condensed
1 bag (16 ounces)	**frozen mixed vegetables,** thawed
1 package (2 count)	**9-inch refrigerated piecrust dough**

Preheat oven to 375 degrees.

Combine chicken, soup, and vegetables. Place one pie shell into pie pan. Spread chicken mixture into pie. Cover with the second crust. Seal edges and make slits in top of crust. Bake 40 minutes, or until crust is golden brown. Makes 4–6 servings.

HAMBURGER VEGETABLE PIE

I pound	**ground beef**
I	**medium onion,** chopped
I can (10.5 ounces)	**condensed vegetable beef soup**
I can (10.5 ounces)	**cream of mushroom soup,** condensed
I tablespoon	**Worcestershire sauce**
3	**medium potatoes,** peeled and cut into small cubes
4	**carrots, peeled and thinly sliced**
¹/₂ teaspoon	**black pepper**
I package (2 count)	**9-inch refrigerated piecrust dough**

Preheat oven to 350 degrees.

In a large frying pan, brown ground beef and onion together until meat is done; drain if necessary. Stir in soups, Worcestershire sauce, potatoes, carrots, and pepper. Divide filling between two 9-inch pie pans. Cover each pie with crusts and tuck crust inside pan's edge. Make slits in top of crusts. Bake 45–50 minutes, or until golden brown. Cool 10 minutes before serving. Makes 8–12 servings.

CHILE RELLENO CASSEROLE

6	**large Anaheim green chiles,** cleaned and diced
1	**large yellow onion,** diced
3 tablespoons	**butter**
6	**corn tortillas,** cut into 1-inch squares
$^1/_2$ teaspoon	**salt**
16 ounces	**Monterey Jack cheese,** grated
4	**large eggs,** at room temperature and separated
1 teaspoon	**cream of tartar**
1 can (10.75 ounces)	**southwest pepper jack soup,** condensed

Preheat oven to 350 degrees.

In a large frying pan over medium-high heat, saute chiles and onion in butter until onion is translucent, about 3 minutes. Add tortilla pieces and saute another 2 minutes. Spread this mixture in a greased 3- to 4-quart baking pan. Sprinkle salt on top. Spread cheese evenly on top. Separate eggs and whip egg whites and cream of tartar until stiff.

In a small saucepan, cook soup and egg yolks over medium heat, stirring constantly until thickened, about 3 minutes. Remove from heat and fold in egg whites. Spread soup mixture on top. Bake 30–40 minutes, or until solid in the center and golden brown on top. Makes 8–10 servings.

HARVEST VEGGIE STUFFING CASSEROLE

1 box (12 ounces)	**seasoned stuffing**
2 cups	**water,** divided
2 cups	**grated zucchini**
1 cup	**diced onion**
1 cup	**grated carrot**
3	**tablespoons butter**
1 can (10.75 ounces)	**cream of mushroom and roasted garlic soup,** condensed
1 cup	**sour cream**

Preheat oven to 350 degrees.

Spray a 9 x 13-inch pan with nonstick cooking spray. Spread stuffing in pan; sprinkle 1 cup water evenly over stuffing. Spread zucchini over top.

In a small frying pan over medium-high heat, saute onion and carrot in butter for about 3 minutes, or until onion is limp. Spread onion and carrot mixture on top of zucchini.

In a small mixing bowl, mix together soup, sour cream, and 1 cup water. Pour on top of casserole and spread with a spoon to make sure edges are sealed. Bake 40–45 minutes, or until bubbly on edges and cooked through in center. Makes 6–8 servings.

POTLUCK POTATOES

I bag (20 ounces)	**frozen seasoned hash brown potatoes**
I can (10.5 ounces)	**cream of chicken soup,** condensed
$^2/_3$ cup	**sour cream**
I cup	**grated cheddar cheese**
$^3/_4$	**medium onion,** chopped

Preheat oven to 375 degrees.

In a bowl, combine all ingredients. Transfer to a greased 9 x 13-inch pan. Bake about I hour, or until bubbly and golden on top. Makes 8 servings.

NEVER-FAIL VEGGIE SOUFFLE

I cup	**steamed and mashed vegetables***
2	**green onions,** chopped
8 ounces	**Swiss or Havarti cheese,** finely grated
I can (10.75 ounces)	**cream of celery soup,** condensed
6	**eggs,** at room temperature and separated
1/2 teaspoon	**nutmeg**
I teaspoon	**cream of tartar**

Preheat oven to 350 degrees.

Whirl vegetables, onion, and cheese in food processor until it resembles coarse crumbles.

In a medium saucepan, cook soup until simmering. Stir in egg yolks and nutmeg and whisk until thickened, about 2 minutes. Remove from heat and stir in vegetable mixture. Whip egg whites and cream of tartar until stiff. Gently fold egg whites into mixture in saucepan. Pour into a 2-quart souffle pan or baking pan that has been oiled on the bottom only. Pour water about 2 inches deep in a large baking pan. Place souffle pan into water in large baking pan. Bake 50–55 minutes. Check to make sure middle is set. When done, turn off oven and let sit about 10 minutes. Makes 4–6 servings.

*Try using steamed spinach, zucchini, butternut squash, broccoli, or cauliflower.

CREAMY PASTA PRIMAVERA

2 tablespoons	**peanut oil**
2 cups	**fresh asparagus pieces** (2-inch)
2 cups	**green onion pieces** (2-inch)
1	**red bell pepper,** cut into julienne strips (2-inch)
2 cans (10.75 ounces each)	**cream of asparagus soup,** condensed
2 tablespoons	**lemon juice**
2 cups	**sour cream**
$^1/_2$ cup	**grated Parmesan cheese**
24 ounces	**penne pasta,** cooked until just tender and drained
2 cups	**fresh spinach,** cut in thin strips
$^1/_2$ cup	**pine nuts or sliced almonds**

In a large frying pan or wok, heat peanut oil and stir fry asparagus, onions, and bell pepper for 2–3 minutes, or until just done. Stir together soup, lemon juice, sour cream, and cheese. Stir soup mixture into vegetables; bring to a simmer. Stir in pasta and spinach and remove from heat. Garnish with nuts and serve warm. Makes 6–8 servings.

FLORENTINE LASAGNA ROLLS

1 box (16 ounces) **lasagna noodles**
1 box (10 ounces) **frozen chopped spinach,** thawed and drained
2 **large eggs,** lightly beaten
1 cup **ricotta cheese**
1/2 cup **grated Parmesan cheese**
1 can (10.75 ounces) **cream of onion soup,** condensed
2 teaspoons **garlic salt**
1 jar (26 ounces) **spaghetti sauce,** divided

Preheat oven to 350 degrees.

Boil lasagna noodles until just tender. Remove from heat and cool.

In a small bowl, mix together remaining ingredients except spaghetti sauce. Pour 1 cup spaghetti sauce in the bottom of a 9 x 13-inch pan. Place a lasagna noodle on a flat surface and spread 1/3 cup spinach mixture on top. Roll up noodle, being careful not to let spinach mixture leak out, making bundles about 4 inches in diameter, with ruffle edges facing out. Place in pan seam side down. Repeat with remaining noodles. Pour remaining spaghetti sauce over top of rolls. Bake 30–40 minutes, or until cooked through and bubbly. Makes 6–8 servings.

CHEESY STUFFED MUSHROOMS

4	**large portobello mushrooms***
4 tablespoons	**canola oil,** divided
I cup	**thinly sliced green onions**
I	**medium tomato,** diced
I box (10 ounces)	**frozen chopped spinach,** thawed and drained
I can (10.75 ounces)	**cream of celery soup,** condensed
1/2 cup	**grated mozzarella cheese**
1/4 cup	**grated Parmesan cheese**
1/2 cup	**seasoned dry breadcrumbs**

Preheat oven to 425 degrees.

Remove stems from mushrooms and clean. Brush mushrooms on all sides with 2 tablespoons oil and then place in a 9 x 13-inch pan.

In a medium frying pan, heat remaining oil and saute onions, tomato, and spinach until liquid has mostly evaporated. Remove from heat and stir in soup and mozzarella cheese. Spoon spinach mixture into caps of mushrooms, mounding and using all the mixture. Bake 15 minutes. Remove from oven. Stir together Parmesan cheese and breadcrumbs. Sprinkle this mixture over the tops of the stuffed mushrooms. Return to oven and broil about 4 inches from broiler for 4–6 minutes, or until topping is golden brown. Makes 4 servings.

*If portobello mushrooms are not available, use about 12 large brown or white button mushrooms.

FAMILY FAVORITE MEAT LOAF

1 1/2 pounds **ground beef**
1 **egg,** beaten
1 cup **sour cream**
2 tablespoons **Worcestershire sauce**
1 envelope **dry onion soup mix**
1/2 cup **grated Parmesan cheese**
1 1/2 cups **seasoned breadcrumbs**
1 can (10.75 ounces) **tomato soup,** condensed

Preheat oven to 375 degrees.

In a large bowl, combine all ingredients except tomato soup. Press meat mixture into a greased 9 x 5-inch bread pan to form a loaf. Spread condensed soup over meat loaf. Bake 55–60 minutes, or until internal temperature reaches 165 degrees. Makes 8 servings.

BREAKFAST OR BRUNCH

CANADIAN BACON AND EGG ENGLISH MUFFINS

1 can (10.5 ounces)	**cream of chicken soup,** condensed
1 cup	**milk**
8	**round slices Canadian bacon**
8	**eggs**
	salt and pepper, to taste
4	**English muffins,** split and toasted

In a saucepan, combine soup and milk over low heat. Heat bacon in a large frying pan until lightly browned on both sides. Remove bacon and cover with foil to keep warm.

In same pan, cook eggs according to personal preference. Season with salt and pepper. Place toasted muffin halves on a serving platter. Layer Canadian bacon and cooked eggs evenly over muffin halves. Spoon hot soup over individual servings. Makes 4–6 servings.

SPINACH AND SAUSAGE BREAKFAST CASSEROLE

I pound	**spicy ground pork sausage**
I bag (6 ounces)	**seasoned small-sized croutons**
4	**eggs**
2^1/$_4$ cups	**milk**
I can (10.5 ounces)	**cream of mushroom soup,** condensed
I package (10 ounces)	**frozen chopped spinach,** thawed
I can (4.5 ounces)	**sliced mushrooms,** drained
I bag (8 ounces)	**grated colby cheese,** divided
^{1}/$_2$ teaspoon	**dry mustard**

Brown, crumble, and drain sausage. Spread croutons over bottom of a greased 9 x 13-inch pan. Spoon cooked sausage over the croutons.

In a bowl, blend eggs and milk. Stir in soup, spinach, mushrooms, I cup cheese, and dry mustard. Pour egg mixture over sausage layer. Sprinkle remaining cheese over top. Refrigerate for 3 hours or overnight.

Preheat oven to 350 degrees. Remove casserole from refrigerator 20 minutes before baking. Bake 50–60 minutes, or until set and browned on top. Makes 8–10 servings.

VEGETARIAN VARIATION: Add a red and green bell pepper in place of sausage.

BREAKFAST PIZZAS

I pound	**ground sausage**
12	**eggs**
$^1/_2$ cup	**milk**
	salt and pepper, to taste
I can (10.5 ounces)	**cream of celery soup,** condensed
2 (12-inch)	**prebaked ready pizza crusts**
$^1/_2$ cup	**real bacon bits**
I	**small onion,** finely chopped
I	**green bell pepper,** seeded and chopped
4 cups	**grated cheddar cheese**

Preheat oven to 400 degrees. Brown, crumble, and drain sausage; set aside.

In a large frying pan, combine eggs, milk, salt, and pepper. Scramble eggs over medium-low heat until firm. Spread $^1/_2$ can soup over each crust. Spoon half the scrambled eggs over each crust. Sprinkle cooked sausage over one and bacon bits over the other. Sprinkle half the onion and bell pepper over each pizza. Top each with 2 cups cheese. Bake 25 minutes, or until golden brown. Makes 12–16 servings.

BAKED HASH BROWN AND HAM CASSEROLE

6	**eggs,** beaten
I teaspoon	**black pepper**
I can (10.5 ounces)	**cream of mushroom soup,** condensed
I cup	**sour cream**
I package (30 ounces)	**frozen country-style hash brown potatoes,** thawed
I	**medium onion,** chopped
I package (16 ounces)	**cooked ham,** cubed
1³/₄ cups	**grated cheddar cheese**

Preheat oven to 350 degrees.

In a large bowl, combine all ingredients. Pour mixture into a greased
9 x 13-inch pan. Bake, uncovered, for I hour, or until set in the center.
Makes 6–8 servings.

CHEESY EGG AND SAUSAGE CASSEROLE

1 tube (16 ounces)	**spicy sausage**
12	**eggs**
1 can (10.5 ounces)	**cream of mushroom soup,** condensed
1¼ cups	**milk**
1 teaspoon	**dry mustard**
½	**medium onion,** chopped
1	**green bell pepper,** seeded and chopped
1 package (30 ounces)	**frozen potato rounds,** partially thawed
1 cup	**grated cheddar cheese**

Preheat oven to 350 degrees. Brown, crumble and drain sausage.

In a large bowl, scramble eggs, soup, milk, and dry mustard. Stir onion, bell pepper, and sausage into egg mixture. Fold in potato rounds. Spread mixture into a greased 9 x 13-inch pan and bake 55 minutes. Sprinkle top with cheese and then bake 10 minutes more, or until cheese is melted and casserole is set. Makes 8–10 servings.

VARIATION: 1 can (4 ounces) drained sliced mushrooms can be added.

MIX 'N' MATCH QUICHE

2	**deep-dish frozen piecrusts,** thawed
I cup	**diced vegetables***
1/2 cup	**cooked diced meat***
2 cups	**grated cheese***
1/2 teaspoon	**spice***
6	**large eggs**
I can (12 ounces)	**evaporated milk**
I can (10.5–10.75 ounces)	**condensed cream soup***

Preheat oven to 350 degrees. Layer in the thawed piecrusts in the following order: vegetables, meat, cheese, and spice.

In a medium bowl, mix together eggs, milk, and soup. Pour into piecrusts, stirring slightly to make sure egg mixture is evenly distributed and there are no air pockets. Bake 45–50 minutes, or until middle of each quiche is firm. Turn off oven and wait another 5 minutes. Serve warm. Makes 2 quiches, 8–10 servings.

*Make choices of any combination that blend well together according to your tastes using these suggested ingredients:

Vegetables: broccoli, cauliflower, green onion, bell pepper, asparagus, and spinach.
Meats: chicken, crab, smoked salmon, ham, sausage, and bacon.
Cheeses: Swiss, Havarti, provolone, Monterey Jack, and Parmesan.
Spices: nutmeg, chili powder, basil, and garlic powder.
Soups: cream of mushroom, celery, asparagus, onion, southwest pepper jack, shrimp, and cheddar.

BAKED BRUNCH ENCHILADAS

2 tablespoons **butter**
$^1/_2$ cup **milk**
12 **large eggs**
2 cups **diced ham**
$^1/_2$ cup **thinly sliced green onions**
1 can (10.75 ounces) **nacho cheese soup,** condensed
1 can (14 ounces) **red or green enchilada sauce**
2 cups **grated cheddar cheese,** divided
10 **medium-sized flour tortillas**

Preheat oven to 350 degrees.

Heat butter in a large frying pan. Mix milk and eggs with a fork and pour into pan. Scramble eggs until done. Stir in ham and onions. Mix together soup and enchilada sauce and then pour 1 cup into a 9 x 13-inch baking pan. Roll a little of the eggs and a little of the cheese in a tortilla, being careful to make sure the same amount is used in all 10 tortillas. Place seam side down in pan. Pour remaining sauce over top. Bake covered 20 minutes. Uncover and bake another 10–15 minutes, or until cooked through and bubbly. Garnish with a little extra cheese. Let stand 5 minutes before serving. Makes 8–10 servings.

HAM AND ASPARAGUS ROLLS

2 cans (10.75 ounces each) **cheddar cheese soup,** condensed
1 1/3 cups **milk**
1/2 cup **grated Parmesan cheese**
1 cup **grated Swiss cheese**
1 teaspoon **garlic powder**
2 cups **cooked rice**
8 slices **cooked ham,** 1/8 inch thick
24 **fresh asparagus spears,** lightly steamed

Preheat oven to 350 degrees.

Combine first five ingredients in a small saucepan and whisk until cheeses are melted and sauce is smooth. Remove from heat. Spread 1/2 cup of the sauce in the bottom of a 9 x 13-inch pan. Mix 1/2 cup sauce into the cooked rice. Lay a slice of ham on cutting board, with longest edge to the front. Spread 1/4 cup of rice mixture on ham slice, leaving 1/2-inch edge all the way around. Place 3 asparagus spears on top of rice. Roll ham slice up like a jellyroll. Place seam side down in pan. Repeat for all ham slices. Pour remaining sauce on top of rolls. Bake 20–30 minutes, or until heated through and sauce is bubbly. Garnish with additional cheese(s) sprinkled on top, if desired. Makes 8 servings.

BAKED GOODS

TOMATO SOUP CAKE

1 box (18 ounces) **spice cake mix**
1 teaspoon **baking soda**
1 can (10.75 ounces) **tomato soup,** condensed
$^1/_2$ cup **water**
$^1/_4$ cup **canola oil**
2 **large eggs**
1 container (16 ounces) **cream cheese frosting**

Combine all ingredients except frosting and beat for 2–3 minutes, or until batter becomes lighter. Bake as directed on back of cake mix box. Cool and frost. Makes 10–12 servings.

VARIATION: Add up to $^1/_2$ cup chopped walnuts, chopped dates, or raisins to batter before baking.

CHEESY MEXICALI CORNBREAD

1 can (10.75 ounces)	**southwest pepper jack soup,** condensed
2	**large eggs,** beaten lightly with a fork
1 cup	**milk**
1 can (4 ounces)	**mild diced green chiles**
2 cups	**frozen corn,** thawed
2 cups	**grated cheddar cheese**
1 1/2 cups	**cornmeal**
1 1/2 cups	**flour**
1 teaspoon	**salt**
1 tablespoon	**baking powder**

Preheat oven to 400 degrees. Spray a 9 x 13-inch baking pan with non-stick cooking spray.

In a large mixing bowl, mix soup, eggs, and milk. Stir in chiles, corn, and cheese.

In a separate bowl, mix dry ingredients together and then add to soup mixture. Pour into pan and spread evenly. Bake 20–25 minutes, or until middle is set and top is lightly browned. Serve warm with butter. Makes 9–12 pieces.

SAVORY MUSHROOM MUFFINS

I can (10.75 ounces)	**cream of mushroom soup,** condensed
$^1/_3$ cup	**milk**
I	**large egg**
$^1/_4$ cup	**melted butter**
4	**white or brown button mushrooms,** cleaned
2 cups	**cake flour**
I tablespoon	**baking powder**
I teaspoon	**garlic salt**
2 tablespoons	**dried parsley flakes**

Preheat oven to 425 degrees.

Place soup, milk, egg, and butter in a food processor or blender. Chop mushrooms in fourths and add to mixture in food processor. Process until smooth and mushrooms are cut into tiny pieces. Pour into a medium-sized mixing bowl. Add dry ingredients and stir until just mixed and no dry streaks remain. Do not over stir. Batter will be slightly lumpy. Spoon batter into greased muffin tins. Bake 20–25 minutes, or until set and lightly browned on top. Makes 12 muffins.

BAKED POTATO BISCUITS

2 1/2 cups **cake flour**
1 tablespoon **baking powder**
1 can (10.75 ounces) **cream of potato soup,** condensed
4 tablespoons **sour cream**
2 tablespoons **water**
1/4 cup **minced chives or green onion tops**
1/2 cup **grated sharp cheddar cheese**
3 tablespoons **cooked crumbled bacon**

Preheat oven to 375 degrees.

In a large mixing bowl, stir together flour, baking powder, soup, sour cream, and water until dough begins to form a ball. Add chives, cheese, and bacon. Turn onto a floured surface and roll out to 1-inch thickness. Cut into 2- to 3-inch circles and place in a pie pan or small baking pan that has been sprayed with nonstick cooking spray. Bake 16–18 minutes, or until lightly browned. Makes about 12 biscuits.

NO-KNEAD FRENCH ONION BREAD

1 1/2 cups	**flour**
2 tablespoons	**sugar**
2 tablespoons	**fast-rising yeast**
1/4 cup	**butter**
1 can (10.75 ounces)	**French onion soup,** condensed
1	**large egg**
1 cup	**grated cheddar cheese**
1 1/2 cups	**whole wheat flour**

In a large mixing bowl, combine regular flour, sugar, and yeast.

In a small saucepan, bring butter and soup to a simmer. Remove from heat and pour into flour mixture. Beat with mixer at medium speed 1 minute. Add egg, cheese, and wheat flour and beat 2 minutes more, or longer until smooth. Spray a large metal bowl with nonstick cooking spray and pour batter into metal bowl. Cover and let rise in a warm place 1 1/2 hours or more, until doubled in size. Grease a loaf pan. Remove from mixing bowl and place in loaf pan. Let rise again until doubled, about 1 hour. Preheat oven to 350 degrees. Bake 50–60 minutes, or until done in center and browned on top.

SWEET POTATO PIE

I can (29 ounces)	**sweet potatoes or yams**
$^1/_4$ cup	**milk**
I can (10.75 ounces)	**tomato soup,** condensed
I cup	**light brown sugar**
3	**large eggs**
I teaspoon	**vanilla**
$^1/_2$ teaspoon	**cinnamon**
$^1/_4$ teaspoon	**nutmeg**
2 (9-inch)	**frozen piecrusts,** thawed

Preheat oven to 350 degrees.

Drain sweet potatoes well and then blend with milk in a food processor or blender until smooth. Pour into a mixing bowl and mix with remaining ingredients except crusts. Pour half the mixture into each crust and bake 60 minutes. Turn off oven and let sit until cooled. Serve at room temperature. Makes 12 servings.

CHOCOLATE ZUCCHINI CAKE

1 1/3 cups **brown sugar**
1/4 cup **butter,** softened
2 **large eggs**
1 can (10.75 ounces) **tomato soup,** condensed
2 cups **pureed zucchini**
2 1/2 cups **flour**
1 tablespoon **baking powder**
2 teaspoons **baking soda**
1 teaspoon **cinnamon**
1/2 cup **cocoa powder**
1/2 cup **diced walnuts**

Preheat oven to 350 degrees.

Cream sugar and butter together. Stir in eggs, soup, and zucchini. Add remaining ingredients, mixing until smooth. Spray a 9 x 13-inch pan with nonstick cooking spray. Pour in batter and bake 30–40 minutes, or until done in center. Cool and frost, if desired. Makes 12 large pieces.

NOTES

NOTES